Why should I study the Quran?

The Holy Quran is not only the Words of Allah but it is also a roadmap to Paradise.

The Holy Quran is a treasure of knowledge and learning that can only enhance our lives and make us better people.

This journal does have sections to help guide you to reflect on the Ayat read, but how many Ayat and how you decide to study is wholly up to you.

O people I am leaving behind among you the Holy Book (Quran) and the Sunnah (way of Prophet (SAW)), if you follow these in letter and spirit you will never be strayed."

This Journal Belongs to:

Study of Surah ------------------

☐ Makki (Revealed in Makkah)

☐ Madani (Revealed in Madinah)

How Many Ayat in This Surah

What are the Themes of this Surah? What does it talk about?

_____

_____

_____

_____

_____

_____

_____

Ayat ____ Thru ____

Summary of these Ayat:

_____

_____

_____

_____

_____

_____

_____

_____

_____

_____

Why were these Ayat revealed:

_____

_____

_____

_____

_____

_____

_____

_____

_____

_____

What did I learn from these Ayat:

_____

_____

_____

_____

_____

_____

_____

_____

_____

_____

_____

Ayah(t) that stand out to me:

_____

_____

_____

_____

_____

_____

_____

_____

_____

_____

How can I apply these Ayat to my life:

_____

_____

_____

_____

_____

_____

_____

_____

_____

_____

Ayat ____ Thru ____

Summary of these Ayat:

_____

_____

_____

_____

_____

_____

_____

_____

_____

_____

Why were these Ayat revealed:

_____

_____

_____

_____

_____

_____

_____

_____

_____

_____

What did I learn from these Ayat:

_____

_____

_____

_____

_____

_____

_____

_____

_____

_____

_____

Ayah(t) that stand out to me:

_____

_____

_____

_____

_____

_____

_____

_____

_____

_____

How can I apply these Ayat to my life:

_____

_____

_____

_____

_____

_____

_____

_____

_____

_____

Ayat ____ Thru ____

Summary of these Ayat:

_____

_____

_____

_____

_____

_____

_____

_____

_____

_____

Why were these Ayat revealed:

_____

_____

_____

_____

_____

_____

_____

_____

_____

_____

What did I learn from these Ayat:

_____

_____

_____

_____

_____

_____

_____

_____

_____

_____

_____

Ayah(t) that stand out to me:

_____

_____

_____

_____

_____

_____

_____

_____

_____

_____

How can I apply these Ayat to my life:

_____

_____

_____

_____

_____

_____

_____

_____

_____

_____

Ayat ____ Thru ____

Summary of these Ayat:

_____

_____

_____

_____

_____

_____

_____

_____

_____

_____

Why were these Ayat revealed:

_____

_____

_____

_____

_____

_____

_____

_____

_____

_____

_____

What did I learn from these Ayat:

_____

_____

_____

_____

_____

_____

_____

_____

_____

_____

_____

Ayah(t) that stand out to me:

_____

_____

_____

_____

_____

_____

_____

_____

_____

_____

How can I apply these Ayat to my life:

_____

_____

_____

_____

_____

_____

_____

_____

_____

_____

_____

Ayat ____ Thru ____

Summary of these Ayat:

_____

_____

_____

_____

_____

_____

_____

_____

_____

Why were these Ayat revealed:

_____

_____

_____

_____

_____

_____

_____

_____

_____

_____

What did I learn from these Ayat:

_____

_____

_____

_____

_____

_____

_____

_____

_____

_____

_____

Ayah(t) that stand out to me:

_____

_____

_____

_____

_____

_____

_____

_____

_____

_____

How can I apply these Ayat to my life:

_____

_____

_____

_____

_____

_____

_____

_____

_____

_____

Ayat ____ Thru ____

Summary of these Ayat:

_____

_____

_____

_____

_____

_____

_____

_____

_____

_____

Why were these Ayat revealed:

_____

_____

_____

_____

_____

_____

_____

_____

_____

_____

What did I learn from these Ayat:

_____

_____

_____

_____

_____

_____

_____

_____

_____

_____

_____

Ayah(t) that stand out to me:

_____

_____

_____

_____

_____

_____

_____

_____

_____

_____

How can I apply these Ayat to my life:

_____

_____

_____

_____

_____

_____

_____

_____

_____

_____

Ayat ____ Thru ____

Summary of these Ayat:

_____

_____

_____

_____

_____

_____

_____

_____

_____

_____

Why were these Ayat revealed:

_____

_____

_____

_____

_____

_____

_____

_____

_____

_____

What did I learn from these Ayat:

_____

_____

_____

_____

_____

_____

_____

_____

_____

_____

_____

Ayah(t) that stand out to me:

_____

_____

_____

_____

_____

_____

_____

_____

_____

_____

How can I apply these Ayat to my life:

_____

_____

_____

_____

_____

_____

_____

_____

_____

_____

Ayat ____ Thru ____

Summary of these Ayat:

_____

_____

_____

_____

_____

_____

_____

_____

_____

_____

Why were these Ayat revealed:

_____

_____

_____

_____

_____

_____

_____

_____

_____

_____

What did I learn from these Ayat:

_____

_____

_____

_____

_____

_____

_____

_____

_____

_____

Ayah(t) that stand out to me:

_____

_____

_____

_____

_____

_____

_____

_____

_____

_____

How can I apply these Ayat to my life:

_____

_____

_____

_____

_____

_____

_____

_____

_____

_____

Ayat ____ Thru ____

Summary of these Ayat:

_____

_____

_____

_____

_____

_____

_____

_____

_____

_____

Why were these Ayat revealed:

_____

_____

_____

_____

_____

_____

_____

_____

_____

_____

What did I learn from these Ayat:

_____

_____

_____

_____

_____

_____

_____

_____

_____

_____

_____

Ayah(t) that stand out to me:

_____

_____

_____

_____

_____

_____

_____

_____

_____

How can I apply these Ayat to my life:

_____

_____

_____

_____

_____

_____

_____

_____

_____

_____

Ayat ____ Thru ____

Summary of these Ayat:

_____

_____

_____

_____

_____

_____

_____

_____

_____

_____

Why were these Ayat revealed:

_____

_____

_____

_____

_____

_____

_____

_____

_____

_____

What did I learn from these Ayat:

_____

_____

_____

_____

_____

_____

_____

_____

_____

_____

_____

Ayah(t) that stand out to me:

_____

_____

_____

_____

_____

_____

_____

_____

_____

_____

How can I apply these Ayat to my life:

_____

_____

_____

_____

_____

_____

_____

_____

_____

_____

Ayat _ _ _ _ Thru _ _ _ _

Summary of these Ayat:

_____

_____

_____

_____

_____

_____

_____

_____

_____

_____

Why were these Ayat revealed:

What did I learn from these Ayat:

_____

_____

_____

_____

_____

_____

_____

_____

_____

_____

_____

Ayah(t) that stand out to me:

_____

_____

_____

_____

_____

_____

_____

_____

_____

_____

How can I apply these Ayat to my life:

_____

_____

_____

_____

_____

_____

_____

_____

_____

_____

Ayat ____ Thru ____

Summary of these Ayat:

_____

_____

_____

_____

_____

_____

_____

_____

_____

_____

Why were these Ayat revealed:

_____

_____

_____

_____

_____

_____

_____

_____

_____

_____

What did I learn from these Ayat:

_____

_____

_____

_____

_____

_____

_____

_____

_____

_____

_____

Ayah(t) that stand out to me:

_____

_____

_____

_____

_____

_____

_____

_____

_____

_____

How can I apply these Ayat to my life:

_____

_____

_____

_____

_____

_____

_____

_____

_____

_____

Ayat ____ Thru ____

Summary of these Ayat:

_____

_____

_____

_____

_____

_____

_____

_____

_____

_____

Why were these Ayat revealed:

_____

_____

_____

_____

_____

_____

_____

_____

_____

_____

What did I learn from these Ayat:

_____

_____

_____

_____

_____

_____

_____

_____

_____

_____

Ayah(t) that stand out to me:

_____

_____

_____

_____

_____

_____

_____

_____

_____

_____

How can I apply these Ayat to my life:

_____

_____

_____

_____

_____

_____

_____

_____

_____

Ayat ____ Thru ____

Summary of these Ayat:

_____

_____

_____

_____

_____

_____

_____

_____

_____

_____

Why were these Ayat revealed:

_____

_____

_____

_____

_____

_____

_____

_____

_____

_____

What did I learn from these Ayat:

_____

_____

_____

_____

_____

_____

_____

_____

_____

_____

_____

Ayah(t) that stand out to me:

_____

_____

_____

_____

_____

_____

_____

_____

_____

_____

_____

How can I apply these Ayat to my life:

_____

_____

_____

_____

_____

_____

_____

_____

_____

_____

Ayat ____ Thru ____

Summary of these Ayat:

_____

_____

_____

_____

_____

_____

_____

_____

_____

_____

_____

Why were these Ayat revealed:

_____

_____

_____

_____

_____

_____

_____

_____

_____

_____

What did I learn from these Ayat:

_____

_____

_____

_____

_____

_____

_____

_____

_____

_____

_____

Ayah(t) that stand out to me:

_____

_____

_____

_____

_____

_____

_____

_____

_____

_____

How can I apply these Ayat to my life:

_____

_____

_____

_____

_____

_____

_____

_____

_____

_____

Ayat ____ Thru ____

Summary of these Ayat:

_____

_____

_____

_____

_____

_____

_____

_____

_____

_____

Why were these Ayat revealed:

_____

_____

_____

_____

_____

_____

_____

_____

_____

_____

What did I learn from these Ayat:

_____

_____

_____

_____

_____

_____

_____

_____

_____

_____

_____

Ayah(t) that stand out to me:

_____

_____

_____

_____

_____

_____

_____

_____

_____

_____

How can I apply these Ayat to my life:

_____

_____

_____

_____

_____

_____

_____

_____

_____

_____

Ayat ____ Thru ____

Summary of these Ayat:

_____

_____

_____

_____

_____

_____

_____

_____

_____

_____

Why were these Ayat revealed:

_____

_____

_____

_____

_____

_____

_____

_____

_____

_____

What did I learn from these Ayat:

_____

_____

_____

_____

_____

_____

_____

_____

_____

_____

Ayah(t) that stand out to me:

_____

_____

_____

_____

_____

_____

_____

_____

_____

_____

_____

How can I apply these Ayat to my life:

_____

_____

_____

_____

_____

_____

_____

_____

_____

_____

Ayat ____ Thru ____

Summary of these Ayat:

_____

_____

_____

_____

_____

_____

_____

_____

_____

_____

Why were these Ayat revealed:

_____

_____

_____

_____

_____

_____

_____

_____

_____

_____

What did I learn from these Ayat:

_____

_____

_____

_____

_____

_____

_____

_____

_____

_____

_____

Ayah(t) that stand out to me:

_____

_____

_____

_____

_____

_____

_____

_____

_____

_____

How can I apply these Ayat to my life:

_____

_____

_____

_____

_____

_____

_____

_____

_____

_____

Ayat ____ Thru ____

Summary of these Ayat:

_____

_____

_____

_____

_____

_____

_____

_____

_____

_____

Why were these Ayat revealed:

_____

_____

_____

_____

_____

_____

_____

_____

_____

_____

_____

What did I learn from these Ayat:

_____

_____

_____

_____

_____

_____

_____

_____

_____

_____

_____

Ayah(t) that stand out to me:

_____

_____

_____

_____

_____

_____

_____

_____

_____

_____

How can I apply these Ayat to my life:

_____

_____

_____

_____

_____

_____

_____

_____

_____

_____

Ayat ____ Thru ____

Summary of these Ayat:

_____

_____

_____

_____

_____

_____

_____

_____

_____

_____

Why were these Ayat revealed:

_____

_____

_____

_____

_____

_____

_____

_____

_____

_____

What did I learn from these Ayat:

_____

_____

_____

_____

_____

_____

_____

_____

_____

_____

_____

Ayah(t) that stand out to me:

_____

_____

_____

_____

_____

_____

_____

_____

_____

_____

How can I apply these Ayat to my life:

_____

_____

_____

_____

_____

_____

_____

_____

_____

_____

Ayat ____ Thru ____

Summary of these Ayat:

_____

_____

_____

_____

_____

_____

_____

_____

_____

_____

_____

Why were these Ayat revealed:

_____

_____

_____

_____

_____

_____

_____

_____

_____

_____

What did I learn from these Ayat:

_____

_____

_____

_____

_____

_____

_____

_____

_____

_____

_____

Ayah(t) that stand out to me:

_____

_____

_____

_____

_____

_____

_____

_____

_____

_____

How can I apply these Ayat to my life:

_____

_____

_____

_____

_____

_____

_____

_____

_____

_____

Ayat ____ Thru ____

Summary of these Ayat:

_____

_____

_____

_____

_____

_____

_____

_____

_____

_____

Why were these Ayat revealed:

What did I learn from these Ayat:

_____

_____

_____

_____

_____

_____

_____

_____

_____

_____

_____

Ayah(t) that stand out to me:

_____

_____

_____

_____

_____

_____

_____

_____

_____

_____

How can I apply these Ayat to my life:

_____

_____

_____

_____

_____

_____

_____

_____

_____

_____

Ayat ____ Thru ____

Summary of these Ayat:

_____

_____

_____

_____

_____

_____

_____

_____

_____

_____

Why were these Ayat revealed:

_____

_____

_____

_____

_____

_____

_____

_____

_____

_____

What did I learn from these Ayat:

Ayah(t) that stand out to me:

_____

_____

_____

_____

_____

_____

_____

_____

_____

_____

How can I apply these Ayat to my life:

_____

_____

_____

_____

_____

_____

_____

_____

_____

_____

Ayat ____ Thru ____

Summary of these Ayat:

_____

_____

_____

_____

_____

_____

_____

_____

_____

_____

Why were these Ayat revealed:

_____

_____

_____

_____

_____

_____

_____

_____

_____

_____

What did I learn from these Ayat:

_____

_____

_____

_____

_____

_____

_____

_____

_____

_____

_____

Ayah(t) that stand out to me:

_____

_____

_____

_____

_____

_____

_____

_____

_____

_____

How can I apply these Ayat to my life:

_____

_____

_____

_____

_____

_____

_____

_____

_____

_____

Ayat ____ Thru ____

Summary of these Ayat:

_____

_____

_____

_____

_____

_____

_____

_____

_____

_____

Why were these Ayat revealed:

_____

_____

_____

_____

_____

_____

_____

_____

_____

_____

What did I learn from these Ayat:

_____

_____

_____

_____

_____

_____

_____

_____

_____

_____

_____

Ayah(t) that stand out to me:

_____

_____

_____

_____

_____

_____

_____

_____

_____

_____

How can I apply these Ayat to my life:

_____

_____

_____

_____

_____

_____

_____

_____

_____

_____

Ayat ____ Thru ____

Summary of these Ayat:

_____

_____

_____

_____

_____

_____

_____

_____

_____

_____

Why were these Ayat revealed:

_____

_____

_____

_____

_____

_____

_____

_____

_____

_____

What did I learn from these Ayat:

_____

_____

_____

_____

_____

_____

_____

_____

_____

_____

_____

Ayah(t) that stand out to me:

_____

_____

_____

_____

_____

_____

_____

_____

_____

_____

How can I apply these Ayat to my life:

_____

_____

_____

_____

_____

_____

_____

_____

_____

_____

Ayat ____ Thru ____

Summary of these Ayat:

_____

_____

_____

_____

_____

_____

_____

_____

_____

_____

Why were these Ayat revealed:

_____

_____

_____

_____

_____

_____

_____

_____

_____

_____

What did I learn from these Ayat:

_____

_____

_____

_____

_____

_____

_____

_____

_____

_____

_____

Ayah(t) that stand out to me:

_____

_____

_____

_____

_____

_____

_____

_____

_____

_____

How can I apply these Ayat to my life:

_____

_____

_____

_____

_____

_____

_____

_____

_____

_____

Ayat ____ Thru ____

Summary of these Ayat:

_____

_____

_____

_____

_____

_____

_____

_____

_____

_____

Why were these Ayat revealed:

_____

_____

_____

_____

_____

_____

_____

_____

_____

_____

What did I learn from these Ayat:

_____

_____

_____

_____

_____

_____

_____

_____

_____

_____

_____

Ayah(t) that stand out to me:

_____

_____

_____

_____

_____

_____

_____

_____

_____

_____

How can I apply these Ayat to my life:

_____

_____

_____

_____

_____

_____

_____

_____

_____

_____

Ayat ____ Thru ____

Summary of these Ayat:

_____

_____

_____

_____

_____

_____

_____

_____

_____

_____

Why were these Ayat revealed:

_____

_____

_____

_____

_____

_____

_____

_____

_____

What did I learn from these Ayat:

_____

_____

_____

_____

_____

_____

_____

_____

_____

_____

Ayah(t) that stand out to me:

_____

_____

_____

_____

_____

_____

_____

_____

_____

_____

How can I apply these Ayat to my life:

_____

_____

_____

_____

_____

_____

_____

_____

_____

_____

Ayat ____ Thru ____

Summary of these Ayat:

_____

_____

_____

_____

_____

_____

_____

_____

_____

_____

Why were these Ayat revealed:

_____

_____

_____

_____

_____

_____

_____

_____

_____

_____

What did I learn from these Ayat:

_____

_____

_____

_____

_____

_____

_____

_____

_____

_____

_____

Ayah(t) that stand out to me:

_____

_____

_____

_____

_____

_____

_____

_____

_____

_____

How can I apply these Ayat to my life:

_____

_____

_____

_____

_____

_____

_____

_____

_____

_____

Ayat _ _ _ _ Thru _ _ _ _

Summary of these Ayat:

_____

_____

_____

_____

_____

_____

_____

_____

_____

Why were these Ayat revealed:

_____

_____

_____

_____

_____

_____

_____

_____

_____

_____

What did I learn from these Ayat:

_____

_____

_____

_____

_____

_____

_____

_____

_____

_____

_____

Ayah(t) that stand out to me:

_____

_____

_____

_____

_____

_____

_____

_____

_____

_____

How can I apply these Ayat to my life:

_____

_____

_____

_____

_____

_____

_____

_____

_____

_____

Ayat ____ Thru ____

Summary of these Ayat:

_____

_____

_____

_____

_____

_____

_____

_____

_____

_____

Why were these Ayat revealed:

_____

_____

_____

_____

_____

_____

_____

_____

_____

_____

What did I learn from these Ayat:

_____

_____

_____

_____

_____

_____

_____

_____

_____

_____

_____

Ayah(t) that stand out to me:

_____

_____

_____

_____

_____

_____

_____

_____

_____

_____

How can I apply these Ayat to my life:

_____

_____

_____

_____

_____

_____

_____

_____

_____

_____

Ayat ____ Thru ____

Summary of these Ayat:

_____

_____

_____

_____

_____

_____

_____

_____

_____

_____

Why were these Ayat revealed:

_____

_____

_____

_____

_____

_____

_____

_____

_____

_____

What did I learn from these Ayat:

_____

_____

_____

_____

_____

_____

_____

_____

_____

_____

_____

_____

Ayah(t) that stand out to me:

_____

_____

_____

_____

_____

_____

_____

_____

_____

_____

How can I apply these Ayat to my life:

_____

_____

_____

_____

_____

_____

_____

_____

_____

_____

Ayat ____ Thru ____

Summary of these Ayat:

_____

_____

_____

_____

_____

_____

_____

_____

_____

_____

Why were these Ayat revealed:

_____

_____

_____

_____

_____

_____

_____

_____

_____

_____

_____

What did I learn from these Ayat:

_____

_____

_____

_____

_____

_____

_____

_____

_____

_____

_____

Ayah(t) that stand out to me:

_____

_____

_____

_____

_____

_____

_____

_____

_____

_____

How can I apply these Ayat to my life:

_____

_____

_____

_____

_____

_____

_____

_____

_____

_____

Ayat _____ Thru _____

Summary of these Ayat:

_____

_____

_____

_____

_____

_____

_____

_____

_____

_____

Why were these Ayat revealed:

_____

_____

_____

_____

_____

_____

_____

_____

_____

_____

What did I learn from these Ayat:

_____

_____

_____

_____

_____

_____

_____

_____

_____

_____

_____

Ayah(t) that stand out to me:

_____

_____

_____

_____

_____

_____

_____

_____

_____

_____

How can I apply these Ayat to my life:

_____

_____

_____

_____

_____

_____

_____

_____

_____

_____

_____

Ayat ____ Thru ____

Summary of these Ayat:

_____

_____

_____

_____

_____

_____

_____

_____

_____

_____

Why were these Ayat revealed:

_____

_____

_____

_____

_____

_____

_____

_____

_____

_____

What did I learn from these Ayat:

_____

_____

_____

_____

_____

_____

_____

_____

_____

_____

_____

Ayah(t) that stand out to me:

_____

_____

_____

_____

_____

_____

_____

_____

_____

_____

_____

How can I apply these Ayat to my life:

_____

_____

_____

_____

_____

_____

_____

_____

_____

_____

Ayat ____ Thru ____

Summary of these Ayat:

_____

_____

_____

_____

_____

_____

_____

_____

_____

_____

Why were these Ayat revealed:

_____

_____

_____

_____

_____

_____

_____

_____

_____

_____

What did I learn from these Ayat:

_____

_____

_____

_____

_____

_____

_____

_____

_____

_____

_____

Ayah(t) that stand out to me:

_____

_____

_____

_____

_____

_____

_____

_____

_____

_____

How can I apply these Ayat to my life:

_____

_____

_____

_____

_____

_____

_____

_____

_____

_____

Ayat ____ Thru ____

Summary of these Ayat:

_____

_____

_____

_____

_____

_____

_____

_____

_____

_____

Why were these Ayat revealed:

_____

_____

_____

_____

_____

_____

_____

_____

_____

_____

What did I learn from these Ayat:

_____

_____

_____

_____

_____

_____

_____

_____

_____

_____

_____

Ayah(t) that stand out to me:

_____

_____

_____

_____

_____

_____

_____

_____

_____

_____

How can I apply these Ayat to my life:

_____

_____

_____

_____

_____

_____

_____

_____

_____

_____

Ayat ____ Thru ____

Summary of these Ayat:

_____

_____

_____

_____

_____

_____

_____

_____

_____

_____

Why were these Ayat revealed:

_____

_____

_____

_____

_____

_____

_____

_____

_____

_____

What did I learn from these Ayat:

_____

_____

_____

_____

_____

_____

_____

_____

_____

_____

_____

Ayah(t) that stand out to me:

_____

_____

_____

_____

_____

_____

_____

_____

_____

_____

How can I apply these Ayat to my life:

_____

_____

_____

_____

_____

_____

_____

_____

_____

_____

Made in the USA
Middletown, DE
26 March 2022

63223788R00116